Res Burman's Poetry
Volume 3

WEI T'O

Protector of Books.

Insures against fire, destructive insects

and

dishonest borrowers.

RES J F BURMAN

Writers' Champion

Copyright © Res J. F Burman 2023
For information contact via email: res.burman@outlook.com

All text materials taken from John's on line blog: http://resswritingandpoetry.blogspot.co.uk

Published through Writers' Champion imprint of MAPublisher (Penzance)
www.mapublisher.org.uk, email: mapublisher@yahoo.com
Printed in UK, April 2023

ISBN-13: 978-1-910499-94-8

Disclaimer:
All expressions and opinions of the work belong to the artists/writer and WC does not share or endorse any other than to provide the open platform to publish their work. For further information on WC policies please email: above email for further information and for submission guidelines.

Book layout, typesetting and cover designed by Mayar Akash
Cover image by Res J. F. Burman
Typeset in Times Roman

Paper printed on is FSC Certified, lead free, acid free, buffered paper made from wood-based pulp. Our paper meets the ISO 9706 standard for permanent paper. As such, paper will last several hundred years when stored.

Content

Introduction

Res Burman is what I call a "Vast" person. He is a person who in his personality, his interests, his experiences, his perceptions, and his talents takes in much of this world in which we live. He has a deep understanding of the human condition combined with the ability to express his understanding with a clear, compassionate, poetic language to which we all can relate.

Res has worked in various professions which include two that might seem poles apart. He was a soldier overseas for a number of years in Her Majesty's service. His interest in and curiosity about the places where he served combined with his natural compassion led him to not only take great interest in the cultures but also to get to know, understand, and care for the people. These experiences made Res a man of the Eastern World as well as a man of the Western World. This gives his poetry its distinctive flavour.

Res has also worked in the profession of animal husbandry. He has a wide-ranging knowledge, understanding, and love of animals, both domesticated and wild. The subject of his poetry often deals with mankind's relationship with animals and our inner-dependence with them. His poetic images often express the human need for a relationship with the animal kingdom and all of nature, emphasizing the importance of an appreciation of the beauty and power of the natural world which so often has a spiritual nature.

Res has lived a life that has combined both the spiritual as well as the practical. Working as a carpenter he has been able to bring together his craftsmanship with his artistic perceptions as a cabinet maker.

The ruggedly beautiful ocean shoreline of Cornwall and the Penzance area have provided a backdrop that has inspired his poetic musings for many years and, more recently, another of his artistic hobbies, photography.

His poems range in motif from the especially serious subject of the spiritual world all the way to a satirical sense of humour expressing thoughts about the absurdities of life. As I think of Robert Frost to be the "American Poet" whose poetry touches on ideas to which all humans can relate, so I think of Res as being the "English Poet" whose poems are wide ranging and express ideas to which all humans can relate. Res is truly the gentlemanly, pirate, Poet of Penzance.

James Wesley
Farmer...Singer/songwriter, poet and writer of prose, teacher, and 1st Mate to Cap'n Res Burman

"We've salt in our veins
And there's tar on our hands
Let's once more away
And seek foreign lands.

And if I find I'm too old
Or I do not have the means
I will still sail the oceans
On a ship of my dreams!"

On Facebook, I used to go by the alias of Driftwood, definitely I could always relate to the ship of the dreams of my friend for over a decade, Res Burman. Connecting over this social media and virtual space, I have always felt a soul connect with Res. We share many common interests some of them undefinable like being seasoned fellow veterans of different Armies, having seen action in different eras and geographical regions, a bond deeper than East meets West.

"I've danced with Death a time or two
And so far come off best
But there's no kind of certainty
That I'll always pass the test.
I've skirmished with the best of 'em
Picked up a scar or two
Had a close encounter with a bayonet
But it didn't run me through."

We may not have bled together, but there is a deep understanding that no matter the varying motifs or colours on our flags, we bleed the same crimson colour.

Poems of Res are like a breath of fresh air, unpretentious and lucid. The wise old man has imbibed an immense wealth of Eastern philosophy and blended it dexterously with his rational western approach.

Res is uninhibited when his poems explore nature and seasons.

"God's Canvas" a tanka
"The view this morning
Was misty and grey... as though
It was God's canvas

Waiting for the Holy Hand
To paint Her Glory upon it"

Res experiments boldly with Haiku and tanka, and is able to deliver the essence of each of these styles. Another recurring theme in many of his poems are nature and seasons and how they affect the fragility of humans

"Autumn airs bring a chill
To my old bones
And my left foot
Which has no feeling
Or big toe nail.... aches!"

The overwhelming sense of aloneness, of loss, finds voice in poems of Res, not as a scream or whimper but simply as a stated fact.

"Someone gave us silver
And took all our colour
In exchange"

Res has been a military veteran and has an inimitable bonding with dogs. We share this mutual love and respect for dogs as man's best friend.

"Lantern hanging in the trees,
Full moon overhead,
An orange moon, a bloody moon,
As I buried my dead!

She'd been a lover for many a year,
A friend so true and brave,
But under that bloody moon
I slaved to dig her grave.

Lantern hanging in the trees,
Full moon looks down scowling
An orange moon, a bloody moon,
I swear I heard it howling!"
I placed some stones above her,
And marked it with a log,
And whispered to her, as oft before,
"Lobo. Stay. Good Dog!"

There is so much more to read, absorb and relish in the poems of "Old Soldier, Traveller, Herdsman, Cow-lifter, Builder, Forester, Carpenter, Cabinetmaker, Woodturner, War Pensioner, Father, Taoist, Photographer, Poet, Lover, Res Burman.

Happy reading, folks.

Lt Colonel Shyam Sunder Sharma, Shaurya Chakra (Retired)
India, War Wounded & Decorated Veteran, Poet, Birdwatcher and Nature lover.

~~~~~~

You're holding in your hands a collection of the poems of Res J.F. Burman, an old soldier, a world traveler, a Taoist, a father, a photographer, a wood-turner, and a man known by many as the Pirate of Penzance. Res is a man who is beloved by many readers in far-flung places, one who has outlived his contemporaries and now faces the loneliness of life's later years with courage and grace.

Res writes of what he knows. Whether commenting on his war experiences, his luck and blessings in love, his encounters with Leonard Cohen in London, his time in Matala in Greece where a young Joni Mitchell found inspiration leading to her masterful Blue album, Res reveals the gentle mastery of a man who has seen a lot and written of it humbly, with heart and wisdom. And when he speaks of his pain and fury, addressing challenges and injustices, Res does so with authority.

Where Res lives in Penzance he has a unique and steadfast view of the world, of the sea and the changing skies. He celebrates the glories and mercies of his days through writing and photography, sharing them across the globe with people who've come to know and love his work. This book is a testament to his goodness and talents, a book that marks a victory of the human kind, a survival of storms, a man's ongoing search for meaning, for what truly matters in life.

Doug Lang
Vancouver, Canada Musician, Prairie Poet and Radio DJ at "Better Days" and "Riverside Drive" on Vancouver Co-op Radio.

Res is a national treasure and this spills forth in his poetry telling of life, love, bygone times and of his many adventures.

His strong compassion for his fellow man shines throughout and it is obvious that Res is a man with much heart. I'm sure yours will be touched many times while reading his poems.

He has a knack for that and also for bringing alive stories of old with emotions and images vividly painted in all their diversity.

I feel blessed to know Res and privileged to have gained a glimpse into his extraordinary life told through his poetry.

I'm sure you will too.

Tina Purplenblue Clowes Kay.
Hill Walker, Poet and Photographer Extraordinaire.

Res Burman's poetry is like a cool wind, the softest ocean in the summer & a bright blue sky filled with the echo of singing birds. His words surround you like a playful & passionate lover who swims inside your heart and mind.

His biggest fan,

Gina Nemo
Gina Nemo is an American actress, singer, author, poet and marketing executive who had an award-winning role as Dorothy Pezzino in the American television series 21 Jump Street in the 1980s. She runs her own Film Actors School. She is the daughter of jazz musician Henry Nemo.

~~~~~   .

Res Burman. A Londoner, a seasoned soldier, who long ago left the rat race behind for a quite life in Cornwall. I have got to know him through his writing and discovered a man of wisdom and wit! Put in simple terms, Res comes to life on the page. An old pirate now, he brings Cornwall to the page for everyone to read, to delight in, his words, sometimes accompanied by photographs, always giving us a close up view of what he calls Pirate Central! A man of charm and compassion, he has a way of bringing the natural world and the human world together like no other poet. His love for the wild animals and wild places come together on the page in perfect harmony. Crafted to perfection, his poetry is simple, sometimes outrageous, serious, humorous and always so readable. Affection for his natural surroundings, love of his fellow man, a craving for justice and fairness for all, Res Burman is, in my opinion, a go to poet. A man for all occasions. And as I sit here writing this now, I can imagine Res sat at his desk in the window, pen in hand looking out over the rooftops to the sea, the tide sweeping new words over the shoreline of his mind. A wise man, a funny man, a friend, a writer without equal. So, pull up a chair, make yourself comfortable, and lose yourself in the words of this Fine poet. Believe me, you will be glad you did.

Dennis Moriarty
Another Londoner who escaped the rat race for Rural South Wales, Mater Poet

Andy Jolley

Yesterday I sat
Where Neville Shute's father prayed
In that little church at Egloshale
I wonder if he imagined
His son's words would fly around the world
Just as his son did
Uniting Cornwall with Dublin
With Burma and Malaya
And his beloved Australia
And who was
Just like my nephew Andy
Another of Wadebridge's best loved sons

4th January 2012

R.I.P. Andy Jolley 1967 - 2011

Hell Bank Notes

Hell Bank Notes
The afterlife taken care of
Now what about this one

Burning Hell Bank Notes
I'll be a rich man when I'm dead
Think I'll burn some girls now

Don't panic ladies, only paper ones, honest!

18th September 2012

Please Don't 'Go' Here

Some places are just
No Go areas ~ so there
So please don't 'Go' here

18th September 2012

Vote Rope

Did they promise us
A hung parliament... or
Not... wishful think?
Perhaps they'll vote another
Aloowance... this time for hemp!

21.5.2010

This isn't as bloodthirsty as it looks. Just a satirical take on all the predictions of a 'hung parliament' and all the Members of Parliament who were caught inflating their Allowance Claims!

Dry Earth

Feet tread the dry earth
Eyes search the sky for rain clouds
As his fathers did

18th September 2012

Wild Geese

Flight of the Wild Geese
That small nations might be free
Proud tears of Erin

17th September 2012

Tiger Balm Gardens

Tiger Balm Gardens
One captured glance from long ago
Still makes my heart quake

16th September 2012

Stapling Rocks

Here in Cornwall
We get such weather
We often staple
Rocks together!

To make our sea wall
Strong and stout
To keep the tide
And water out.

But sea salt and iron
You can trust
Eventually will
Give way to rust!

So now when our sea wall
We must heal
We put our trust in
Stainless steel!

9th May 2008

Buck Polly

Buck Polly my friend
Another twelve stringer down
The needle of death

18th September 2012

This is the last photograph I ever took of my friend Buck Polly. A promising 12 guitar player. Buck died of an overdose whilst I was overseas. The 'halo' was caused by the reflection of the flash gun in the mirror. I wouldn't like to suggest that Buck was an angel!

Bert Jansch wrote a poignant song about Buck's death entitled "Needle of Death" R.I.P. Buck Polly.

Seagull

Seagull
Like a flying handkerchief
Blown across the bay

20th August 201

Monterey Pines and Cypresses

Pines and cypresses
All the way from Monterey
Thrive in Cornish soil

13th September 2012

Monsoon Water

Monsoon water rising
Cipher machines up on bricks
A canoe ride home

16th September 2012

Monkey See

Monkey see
Monkey do
Monkey bite

1st January 2012

Snake Screamer

Monkey on the fence
Lived in an Anchor Beer crate
Sweet thing ~ Snake screamer

25th August 2012

Shop Houses

I love shop houses
Cool shady five foot walk-ways
Treasures of the East

16th September 2012

Ghosts of Good Dogs

I feel a warm body
Pressed against my leg
Ghosts of good dogs gone

19th January 2012

Kipling

Kipling, I loved him dearly
And in return
He tried to look like me

7th January 2012

Evening Kestrel

Hovering above
The old Fishermen's Chapel
Evening's kestrel flight

1st September 2012

Spring Days - haiku

Oh for those Spring days
When my hair still grew curly
And my smile fitted

1st September 2012

Harvest

(Devon and Cornwall)

The smooth lift and flex
Of muscles… the sheen of sweat
Earning our daily bread

Blossom the cart-horse
Big as an icy mountain
Gentle as a lamb

Harvest ~ honest work
Feeding honest appetites
Winter's sustenance

Harvest Festival
An old sinner like me would sing
Now all is safely gathered in

After the harvest
Arms and back aching from toil
Still the cows to milk

One hundred cows wait
Outside the milking parlour door
I call them name by name

As the evening cools
Cattle share warmth and sweet breath
And milk for my tea

12th September 2012

The English Hawthorn

The English Hawthorn
Queen of the May ~ short stocky
Strong as the earth it springs from

Hawthorn blossom
Seldom heard
Over the sound of casting clouts

13th September 2012

Forgotten Footsteps

This path
Made by forgotten footsteps
Lost in the forest

13th September 2012

East and West

When East and West meet
With music and laughter
Even the Gods smile

13rd September 2012

OM

Quietly humming OM
I walk through a herd of cattle
Disturbing none

31st August 2012

Dreaming of Kuching

Dreaming of Kuching
Like fragrant smoke on the air
Market vendors call

Loved souls reach to caress me
In this land that stole my heart

6th May 2011

The Year of the Water Dragon

The Year of the Water Dragon
Red Envelopes for all the Children
But where are the fire-crackers
To scare away all my ghosts

23rd January 2012

Denver

Denying his age
The eternal child still plays
My old mate Denver

19th August 2012

Dawn

Dawn warms the morning air
Causing updraughts over the sea
Enough to lift my wings

12th February 2012

The Crocodile's Smile

The crocodile's smile
May hide many mysteries
None bode well for me

30th August 2012

This picture, not mine, unfortunately, is reputed to be the skull of the notorious man eating crocodile known as "Bujang Senang", The Happy Batchelor! He haunted the Peleban River in Sarawak, North Borneo in the 1980's and 90's. Dedicated to Mokhtar Sah Malik

Forgotten Dreams

My roof collapsed
No longer supported
By all those forgotten dreams

12th February 2012

Hungry Ghosts

Amitabha Buddha
Reminds me to make offerings
To my hungry ghosts

31st August 2012

Goose On My Shoulder

Goose on my shoulder
Like Long John Silver's Parrot
Three eyes between us

25th August 2012

The Sound of Thunder

These old granite cliffs
Above the waves rolling in
The sound of thunder

1st September 2012

I'd Wait At The Station Forever

My old friend Bonzo
I'd wait at the station forever
If I thought he'd come home

19th August 2012

Blue Horses

Blue Horses stampede
Through Penzance's crowded streets
Festival time again

12th February 2012

Blue Moon

Blue Moon
Cool breeze returns to the woods
The Bamboo shivers

1 September 2012

The Apprentice! A Gull's Tale.

I am young but I am learning
Learning how to make my way
How to make my living
And getting better day by day.

Sometimes hungry, sometimes sated
Sometimes hungry once again
And yes! I'm sometimes raucous
And sometimes I'm a pain!

On land I am a scavenger
Some say a "flying rat"
But I swim upon God's Ocean
Now what do you think of that?

I am young but I am learning
To be accepting of all things
And I can soar just like an angel
With God's wind beneath my wings!

4th August 2008

Exile Tanka

As winter storms in
My little mimosa tree
Sports shivering blooms

The collared dove warms her feet
Dreaming of Southern Sunshine.

Far from the mountains
Where sages lived forever
My heart grows older

Remembering younger days
And weeping dark bamboo tears.

25th November 2009

Milk Fever & Cow Lifting

"Res, I've got a cow down!"
My friend Leonard said,
"Show me, my friend!" said I,
And followed where he led.

Big black and white Friesian
Fallen and wedged quite tight
Behind the feeding troughs
And it was coming on for night!

"Milk fever?" I asked quietly
So as not to fright the cow
"Have you got the calcium in 'er?"
"Yes, I've just done it now!"

"Did you stick it in the milk vein?"
"No, just under the skin!"
"Damn, it'll take forever,
Milk vein's the place to whack it in!"

Though it wasn't Leonard's fault
But it really was a pain
With half a ton of cow on top
You couldn't reach the vein!

"Leonard we'll have to lift 'er,
But there isn't any space,
What have you got in the lifting way
That we can get into this place?"

"Well, I've got a pin-bone clamp,
That I picked up one time,
But nothing in the lifting way
That we can bring on line!"

"Come Leonard, I've seen scaffold poles
Out there in the scrap,
And sheave blocks and grain hoists
We can make something out of that!"

cont.

So we scat a hole up through the floor
Of the granary upstairs,
And built a sheer-legs out of poles
And collected pulley wheels in pairs.

Some rope from the bale trailer,
Threaded through the wheels
And we had a block and tackle
With a four to one lift deal!

So clamp clamped on the pin-bones
And filled with more than hope,,
Two husky sons and I began
To pull down on that rope!

"Oh Res, she's lifting nicely!"
Our Leonard he did say,
But her arse came up and her chin stayed down,
And then she stayed that way!

"No good, no good, no good!" I cried,
"Lower her down once more!
Gently now, don't let her drop!"
And we lowered her to the floor!

"We need another sheer-legs,
We need more rope and blocks,
Send a son to fetch back mine,
The one I use for moving rocks!"

So we built another sheer-legs,
Another hole in the granary floor
We made a sling for under her chest
And we start to lift her more!

This time she came up even
And we held her there a-while
But she wouldn't take her own weight
Not by a country mile.

"We need to massage her legs
To get some feeling back
But there just isn't room to work,
We'll have to lay her back!"

cont.

"No! No!" I said, "Let's tie her off,
Let's make a careful plan,
Let's cut some rollers and a door,
To lay her back upon!"

This we did, we cut some pipes,
We found a fine stout door
And arranged them underneath
Before we lowered her to the floor.

Now inch by inch we dragged her
Backwards on her door,
Until she popped, just like a cork
Onto the loose-box floor.

Ah now we would have room to work,
We let her rest just then.
No rest for us, we had to do
The whole job over again!

Two more holes up through the ceiling
Arrange the sheer-legs and the rope
The clamp, the sling, the blocks and all,
And start again with hope!

This time we raised her neatly
We were getting good by now,
We tied her off just dangling there,
And went to work on the cow.

We massaged each leg carefully,
She really did look sick,
We lifted them and flexed their joints
She was too tired to kick.

We built a wall of straw bales
To hold her up a while
And gradually slacked off the ropes
You should've seen Old Leonard smile.
We were also smiling
As we saw her take her weight
Another cow saved once more
From the Knacker-man's fate.

cont.

And in the lantern light we sat
Mrs L bought tea and scones,
Cow suckled calf, and Len and me
Were weary to our bones.

But satisfied and well pleased
With our labour on that day,
We'd earned a piece of heaven
As we went upon our way

15th July 2008

St Just Fire Brigade

St Just Fire Brigade are volunteers
But when they are called out
The Butcher, Baker and Candlestick maker
All turn out for a "Shout."

One time they put out a fire
In a Penzance Square,
They say they put the fire out
Before Penzance crew got there!

They'd turn out for anything
Cat up a tree, or stuck under a log,
A puppy down a mine shaft
Or a heifer stuck in a bog!

Peter Bennetts prize heifer
Up to her belly in marsh.
And 'im an' his lads couldn't budge 'er
Oh Lord! Peters comments were harsh!
So they called the boys out with their engine
Duckboards and sheer-legs and toys
Slings and sheave blocks for pulling
They knew what they were doin' those boys!

They heaved and they splashed and got muddy
The heifer got frightened and guess,
Yeah, frightened cattle always
Add a good contribution to mess.

Things got smelly and mucky
Neighbours arrived to lend hand
And with much swearin' and sweating
Eventually they got her to land.

Poor heifer stood shaking and trembling
The boys started cleaning their tack
Peter said to his son Johnathan
"Get a bottle of rum! Hurry back!"

All the firemen looked hopefull
And slowed down what they was doin'

cont.

They'd earned a drink of any mans rum
But they didn't know what was ensuein'.

The Firemen all looked thirsty
The bottle arrived like a zephyr
Peter Bennett took one long sniff
An' poured it all down the throat of the Heifer!

Faces have never dropped further
As they watched the gurgling grog
They saved Bennetts heifer that day
But Peter, they threw back in the bog!

25th February 2008

The Beaufort Scale

The Beaufort Scale is an empirical measure for describing wind velocity based mainly on observed sea conditions.

The Beaufort Scale

Without regard for life or limb,
The weather, it comes storming in.
The waves do build, the wind does wail
As the weather climbs the Beaufort Scale.

At Force Six, Strong Breeze, large waves with foam
The fishing fleet starts to think of home
At Seven, Near Gale, the foam does streak
Out-doors is no place for the weak!

At Eight, the waves are eighteen feet,
And cars veer across the street!
At Strong Gale Nine, the slates do fly,
And chimneys shake against the sky.

At Ten, Whole Gale, whole trees do go,
And whole roofs too, "Look out below!"
Force Eleven has thirty seven foot waves,
And has taken many to their graves!

But Force Twelve has another dread name,
And that dread name is hurricane!
Ninety miles an hour winds, sixty foot seas,
Will do with you just what they please!

And wind and wave can go much higher,
If I told you now you'd think me liar!
But in the shriek and wave and wail,
You'll pray to God that you prevail!

And when it's over you won't believe
This friendly breeze knocked you to your knees.
You count your dead, lay them away
And brace to face another day.

But remember when fishers head away,

cont.

And sailors seek a sheltered bay,
When the weather is unfit for all,
The Life-boat is ready for your call!

Those brave, brave men will always sail
No matter what the Beaufort Scale.
They'll do their best for you and me,
And all in peril on the sea!

7th May 2008

Dedicated with the greatest admiration to the Crew of Lifeboat Solomon Browne, who, on the night of 19th December 1981 gave their lives trying to rescue the Crew of the Coaster Union Star. Both Crews were lost.

After one day of searching for survivors or bodies, another full crew of volunteers reported for duty on the replacement lifeboat! I have seen Courage in many guises but have never seen such Courage as this!

Fairy Queen

If you were a Fairy Queen
A crown of Clover would be seen
Upon your head and in your hair
I know because I'd place it there.

I'd scatter bluebells round your feet
And bring honey for you to eat.
I'd ask the birds and ask the bees
To sing you songs and bring you ease.

Robes I'd weave from Mermaids Hair
Scatter roses everywhere
Write songs of you, for others to sing
Were you my Queen and I your King.

Oh yes I know it's make-believe
Like favours sewn upon a sleeve
And heraldry so seldom seen,
But to me you are my Queen.

And though we work and though we play
The magic is not far away
Your lovely hair crowns your lovely head
You bring love and rose petals to my bed.

11th May 2008

Morning Walk

A pretty pastel morning,
The sea a gentle swell,
The morning Sun is climbing,
Over sand and sea and shell.

The air is like cool satin,
A caress against my face,
I stretch my legs and swing my arms,
Picking up the pace.

I want to get to Marazion,
The next town round the bay,
There and back will be five miles,
I hope to keep fit this way.

The light is always changeing,
The scene is always new,
It would take a lifetime,
To tire of this view.

There's rabbits playing on the grass,
And always dogs I know,
They'll remember me for a biscuit,
And bring me balls to throw.

There's flowers there to photograph,
And swans fly over the foam,
And maybe a "bacon banjo",
Before I venture home!

12th May 2008.

Life and Death

A sweet friend who I love dearly
Not halfway through her beauty
Starts to fear for her passing
Starts to fear her dying hour
Will she waste the beauty
Of her loveliness and spirit
By fearing the one thing
That we know will come to pass?

We are all upon a journey
An exciting vivid pathway
Not just from birth to death
But from alpha to omega.
From amoeba to future man
From Africa to America
If we can trace our DNA
To the dawn of time in Africa
Surely by all that's Holy
It must stretch as far the other way!

All of us who have loved someone
Must have felt that consciousness
That expanding of awareness
Beyond the function of the brain!
That knowing beyond thinking
That's the senses of the spirit
That's the knowing that can go with us
When we leave this life behind!

I am quite content to know
The limit of my understanding
Cannot hope to encompass
Everything that will be so.
Whether playing harps in Heaven
Or going walkies with a Dog God
Or worshipping a Goddess
Oh Goddess let it be so!
Or imagine just an energy
With that loving consciousness
Merging with all others that have ever been.
Imagine all the sparking, the laughing and the larking
When this life is over I'll be content to go there.
I'm in no hurry to move onward

cont.

But I know it's surely coming
There's one or two would kick my ass
If I went too soon!
When my time comes I hope
I'm not a miser at my ending
Clinging greedily to days and nights
Whose worth is sadly declining.
But ready to hopefully
Face the onward journey
With all the love I've saved up
In my ever-loving' life!

Someone said 'twas better
To always travel hopefully
Than to arrive.
I think that's a better way
To try to live your life.
Live up to life's promise
Live all your life hopefully
No matter what the setbacks
Love as many dearly
As you'd wish to love yourself
This can be a life of beauty
And your only duty
Is to do your very best
For the best part of your life.

There's no need to live fearfully
Because of what is coming
That is just to waste the thing
That life has given us.
Death is just the next step
In the journey we must travel
To regret any part of it
Is to regret life itself.

So give yourself to living
Give yourself to loving
Give yourself to travelling
This lovely vivid road
Give to travelling hopefully
Till age make travelling wearyfull
Then allow kindly death relieve you of your load.

18th May 2008

This is dedicated to my dear friend Dena with Love and Admiration.

A Pair of Shorts

Raptor

Inspired by John Trudell's lovely song "Raptor"

Dancing in the dark,
To "Raptor"
Fine, fierce, feminine,

Flight of fancy,
Without you!

****

My Familiar Woods

My familiar woods,
Night breezes whisper,
My echo-locator
On the dark path home.

20th May 2008

To Lao Tzu and The Earthquake

To Lao Tzu and The Earthquake

A Message From The West.

You spent your life
Learning and teaching
Serving by being.
Like water content
To take the lower path.
Seeking the common level.
And like water
Moving softly
But wearing away
Mountains of greed,
Ignorance and prejudice
By the practice
Of your faith and
The truth of your words!

As you grew older
Who knows if 'twas
Towards the end
Or the beginning
Of your sacred life,
You abandoned mans greed
And took another pathway.

You mounted your Water Buffalo
Xiao Gao Jiao, Little Longhorn
That most patient of companions
And rode away
Towards the West,
Where your wisdom
Was then so badly needed.
More so than at home.

I have often wondered
When you would get here!
But as you told me in a dream,
To those whose hearts are open,
You are already here.

cont.

Perhaps now, Honoured Friend,
Whilst China's bosom is bleeding
By the Dragon's shrugging shoulders,
So many dead, so many needing comfort.
It is time for you to return
To China once again.

Ah! But of course,
Lao Tzu. Wo lao pen yu,*
To those whose hearts are open,
You are already there!

Take your wisdom and your acceptance
To those in need of understanding.
Join with Lady Kuan Yin,
Bring healing to the sore.
Lay the hand of comfort
Upon the souls of those who suffer,
Grant them the strength to survive
And the wisdom to rebuild.

Tell them that those who see
The Tao. By whatever name
Different peoples give it,
Send their wishes for recovery
And our hopes for days to come,
And their love to share
In both the sorrows and the happiness
Of our brothers and our sisters
In the East and Everywhere!

21st May 2008

A Mother's Sacrifice

A Mothers Sacrifice.

In the Land of the Giant Panda,
In the Province of Sichuan,
They were digging in the rubble,
Still hoping to find someone.

They found a Mother stiff and cold,
How long had she been there,
Dying under the wreckage,
Dust and grit all in her hair.

As they gently turned her over,
Knowing they were too late,
They saw, shielded by her body,
A baby, saved from it's Mothers fate.

A careful Policeman noticed,
The Mother clutching tight,
A cell phone with a text upon it,
The last thing she'd ever write.

"Dear Baby" she had written,
Trapped there in the dark.
"Remember the person who saved you,
And these words you must mark!"

"Make a meaningful life for yourself,
Live so all our neighbours can see,
That you were worthy of my sacrifice,
And an Honourable Son to me!"

22nd May 2008

The Worthy Teacher

The Worthy Teacher.

This heaped up pile of rubble,
This was once the school.
Where The Teacher held his classes,
And taught the Golden Rule.

He took his duties seriously,
He loved to bring the light
Of learning to his pupils,
And taught them wrong from right.

"Be true to yourselves and each other,
Stand up for your fellow man,
Help your brothers and sisters,
And protect all those that you can!"

When the Dragon shook it's shoulders,
And tore their world apart,
There was only one lesson left,
For that worthy Teacher to impart.

Three students he pushed under the platform,
Protected by the overhanging shelf,
And when he couldn't cover the entrance,
He covered it up with himself!

He gripped the edge of the platform,
His fingers locked on so tight,
They had to break his poor dead fingers
When they bought his poor body to light!

But under the platform, protected,
Saved from all flying stone and glass,
Three teenage pupils were found safely,
Where The Teacher had held his last class!

With the vice-like grip of his fingers,
With his blood and his very last sigh,
He proved that the lessons he'd taught them
Were the things for which he would die!

cont.

This is one tale among many,
Of brave people who answered the call,
But the lesson that brave Teacher taught
In his last class, is one for us all!

25th May 2008

This is the last (I think) in my Earthquake Trilogy. I heard of this Teachers courage from the blog of my friend Yang Wei, who works in one of the many hospitals to which badly injured survivors are being evacuated.

The Chinese people in the Sichuan Earthquake Area still need every help we can give them, whether it be money, food, shelter or just prayers and well wishes. Give generously of what you can. Love to all of you ~ Res

The Miracle at Country Life Press Station

There comes a time in many a young life,
After stony roads and loads of strife,
We can fall into places inter-tidal,
Then hopeless we sink to suicidal.

Young girl sitting by the railroad line,
Feelin' she'd just run out of time,
Body and mind shrieked the same refrain,
"I'm gonna end it under the very next train!"

Sitting down the end of Chestnut Street,
Waiting there her fate to meet,
Praying for that final expiation,
On disused Country Life Press Station.

Just sitting there in a world of pain,
Waiting for that lethal train,
She thought she sat all alone there,
When "Got a Smoke?" whispered in her ear!

An old Hobo sat there by her side,
Frightened her so she nearly died,
Then she saw that as a ghastly joke,
So they sat there quiet and shared a smoke.

A train was coming! But she just sat there,
Suicide is a very private affair,
Her innate good manners, she couldn't end
Her life in front of her smoking friend!

The train pulled up, in that screeching way,
"Better get on this one," she heard him say,
"Won't be another chance." he said so mild,
"Thanks for the smoke, God Bless you child!"

She climbed aboard and waved good-bye,
He wasn't there, she didn't know why.
"Tickets please!" said the Conductor Man,
Standing there, holding out his hand.
"I haven't a ticket, I must confess,
Can I buy one from Country Life Press?"   cont.

"You must be mistaken, Child, I greatly fear.
Trains ain't stopped there for many a year!"

She was too shocked to argue the matter,
Her heart was beating pitter-patter,
A pain in her soul like a bowie knife,
Had an Angel Hobo just saved her life?

From that day on she never looked back,
On the smoothest roads or the outward track,
Not once more did she go adrift,
She made good use of the Hobo's Gift.

Young Girl grew up strong and true,
Good friend to me, good neighbour to you,
And the only flaw in her reputation,
Is a belief in Angels on a disused station!

26th May 2008

This is a true story that happened many years ago while Country Life Press Station, Long
Island was closed, though trains still whistled through!

The Servants Reply

The Servant's Reply

I am Restless, breathless with desire,
Your studies have my skin on fire,
Each touch and slide with hand or knee,
Are fuelling fires deep in me.
I feel your gaze as you take in,
Every line from toe to chin.
I feel your breath upon my skin,
It makes my senses reel and spin.
I wouldn't stop, I wouldn't wait,
There stands a Queen at my gate.
Oh Welcome, welcome, come inside,
I pray that you have come to 'bide.
Explore my body search my mind,
There's love here, love, for you to find.
Aye Love and Lust in equal measure,
Give me, take me, equal pleasure.
Pleasure me, love me, once, again,
The perfect potion for all pain.
And let this be a flowing sea,
Between the shores of thee and me.
There's nothing that you may not ask,
Pleasure, pain or worthy task.
And after lust is all assuaged,,
And you lie with bed and legs dis'rayed.
Come back to love and love me sweet,
You'll be my wine, you'll be my meat.
You'll be my love, my heart and Queen.
Like no love that's before been seen.
Let's build a love as bright as day,
And pray it never, ever fades away.

I should point out that Servant in this case means one who serves, not necessarily one who is subservient. It is also a play upon my surname which in Old English originally meant "A Servant in the Bower" or "He who serves in a Noble Lady's Bed Chamber." Eat you heart's out Guys - Lucky Me!

1st January 2008

Heart Attack

Some time ago, through exertion, stress and probably the wrong medication I thought I was having a heart attack. Do not worry about this, certain things went wrong and I have sorted them since. Nothing to worry about.

However, I was at the top of Causwayhead, in Penzance and feeling a bit crook, so I stopped at Sean's Diner, sat at a picnic table outside and ordered a pot of tea. I was a little shaky and having chest pains so I decided that with the tea I'd take an aspirin, SOP.

The tea came and I searched my bag for the aspirin I knew was there. Now there are many pockets in my bag and there is something in nearly every one of them. But no aspirin!

Oh shit, search more carefully, this takes a while, feeling worse, no bloody aspirin. Sean came to the door of the cafe to say, "Hi." By this time I was visibly shaking and sweat was running down my face and down my back. "Sean. Have you any aspirin?" said I urgently. "Nah. You'll get some at the bottom of the street at the Newsagents." he replied casually, turning and sauntering back to his kitchen. I thought, "Sod it, woulda done ya good to run down there for me." But of course, ever the good Taoist, I bit my tongue.

Across the street, Sweeny Todd's the Barber Shop, all the girls in there know me, they all know I have a bit of heart trouble, they'll help. I walked to the door, my shirt by now drenched with sweat, shaking and clutching my chest, raucous laughter, Essex girls chatting quietly, "Has anyone got an aspirin!" I shouted over the row. "Nah, but I've got asthma, if that's any good to ya!" A voice shouted back. "Huh!" I thought, "If I'd offered a bit of leg-over you'd have shown more interest!"

Now, I've danced with death a time or two and it doesn't hold any more fears for me than the next man, but if I'm gonna go, I'd like a little more warning than a goddam big finger pointing down at me from the sky and saying "Now". Besides, there were things left undone. And I thought it would be bloody stupid to die now for want of a tuppeny ha'penny aspirin!

So off I set, down the hill heading for the newsagent. Staggering a little by now, still clutching my chest and shaking quite badly. Vaguely aware of glances but no help at hand. By now I'm thinking to myself, "I could die here and no bugger would even notice. I'd probably be lying here till the Road Sweepers turned up!" This seemed totally unacceptable so I became even more determined to survive this brush with the Grim Reaper.

Finally I made it to the door of the Newsagents. McNews, members of that old Scottish Clan of Stationers and Newsagents. But what's this? Stuck in the doorway, two sweet old ladies. "Now Dear, shall I go in and get ... while you go elsewhere and get... or shall we both go in.... and go elsewhere after together...etc etc. Do you know how long an et cetera can become when you're having a heart attack?

Now it did occur to me to shout, "Get out of the f*cking way, I'm having a heart attack!" Of course I realised that this could confuse the issue more, and what right did I, as a good Taoist, have to shout at two little old dears anyway. All this I considered, while jumping from foot to foot, not deliberately, the shakes had developed into the sort of macabre gyrations of St Vitas Dance. Could I shout at two little old ladies? F*cking right, I could. I filled my lungs, to capacity!

It was then, a Damascus Road revelation. Oh God/dess. Knowing my luck I'd just get to shouting! And the Golden Gates would crash open and I'd tumble through yelling, "Get out of the f*cking way!"

Well. Imagine it. You'd be able to hear an angels feather fall to the fluffy cloud floor, wouldn't you? Oh Shit, the disgrace, especially when you were there for the long haul. An' there's me wanting to be a Saint, but not till a half hour before kick-off, if ya catch my drift.

So I dithered while the old ladies dithered, and then they moved. Leap for the gap, slip through, and there's Michelle.

Ah Michelle, daughter of the McNews Clan, pretty as a picture, she'll help, born for the role of Angel of Mercy. "Michelle, Michelle, have you any Aspirin?" - - - "Yes," nonchalantly, "Up the end of the shop!" Turning away. Jesus, McNews is the longest shop in Penzance, I can barely see to the other end.

I stagger on, this is now like a marathon, oh bugger, there's two steps up too. Up clump thud Up clump thud. My two legs and my walking stick making a three point tempo to accompany the thudding of my heart and the pounding of my pulse.
My vision clears slightly as I near the counter, now is the time for multi-tasking if ever I knew one, so I am now pulling handfuls of loose change out of my pocket, pennies and five penny pieces rolling everywhere, I get to the counter, "Aspirin, Aspirin, gimme some Aspirin!" I shout in a cracked hoarse voice filled with the urgency of a dying man.

"You just wait your turn like everyone else Dear," was the reply, "I'll be with you when I've served this lady!" One of the little old dears from the door had beaten me to the counter. How the f*ck had she done that? I had galloped up that damn shop!

There are those in this world who actually go slower when there is urgency in the air. Yes, I had one of those. Finally, my turn, "Aspirin you want, do you Dear?" By this time I'm practically inarticulate, "Yessssss." I hiss urgently through the rigor of my clenched teeth. Oh! Sweet Jesus, they are at least three feet away, how many steps can you fit into three feet? And they are on the top shelf, two tries to reach them. Ah, she has them in her hand. "I've got Aspirin..." I cannot believe my eyes as she puts them back and picks up the next packet, "And I've got paracet..." "Gimme the Aspirin" I shriek suddenly finding my voice.

She puts the paracetamol back on the shelf, and yes, has two grabs at the aspirin before grasping it. She brings it closer, I lean over the counter to grab it from her hands. She holds it tantalizingly out of reach, "Now wait a minute Dear, You know I've got to scan it first!"

Finally it is within reach, I grab the little box while shoving the pile of loose change towards her. I scrabble with the box, out fall the bloody instructions, do I need these, I think not! Ah! The blister pack, I push one tablet through the tinfoil and toss it to the back of my throat. Quick draw of my water bottle and swig it down. Ah! Saved..... Oh Shit! Shouldn't have necked it, won't dissolve in time. Struggle to get another tablet out of the blister pack. Throw that one in, chew madly, mouth dry, bits of aspirin flying with each exhalation through my gasping mouth, chew chew drink swallow. Phew!

"Have you got a really bad headache Dear?" says the slow lady behind the counter!

Taoist wisdom prevents me immolating her with my glare. I shuffled out to the bench in the street outside and ponder the near Golden Gate experience and it was then that I had my second Road to Damascus moment of the Day.

If I had burst through the gates to be faced with a Man who had promised to love me unconditionally and forgive me all my sins, a responsibility I had always shouldered myself, would I have been able to cope with that. I don't think so. So where could I look for unconditional love and forgiveness?

And then I knew. I saw it all. My enlightenment. All questions answered. Yes I can see it now!

I'd walk in those ol' golden gates and up there on the comfy cushion , pleased as punch to see me. The biggest loveliest DOG you could imagine. Bounding down, jumping up, knocking me down, which wouldn't matter 'cos the grass in Heavens gotta be clean and soft eh? And all my joints would be renewed and supple so landing hard wouldn't matter. And that Ol' Dog would wag and wriggle and I would dig my fingers in his fur and scratch and stroke and tickle and he would lick and forgive me all my sins and love me forever! Who else could do that?

When I die I'm gonna be head down and runnin' at them gates. "Here boy! Here boy! Let me in! I'm a-comin' home. Walkies!"

3rd January 2008

Cultivating Love and Fruit
(Parental Advisory)

Cultivating Love and Fruit

Hail, my lady, I stand proudly
In your presence here
I come to polish apples
And plant my seeds down there!

I am intent on cultivation
Is this fertile earth and fresh
Watered by my salivation
To bring sweetness from your flesh?

Oh your apples shine so sweetly
In the candle light of night
And the pips pucker to my touch
Oh you are a lovely sight.

I love your scent I love your taste
I love your peachy skin
I love the splitting of the fig
As you rise to let me in.

But first a salty furrow
I'd plough with tongue and nose
I'll tip-toe through your tulips
Now who's got curling toes?

I see your nectar oozing
I see this earth rise up
I love your taste I love your scent
Drinking from your loving cup.

I peel your grape
And taste it there
Oh thou art, thou art,
Thou are fair!

And now comes time
To stir the spell
Mixed in this cauldron

cont.

I love so well.
Pestle in mortar
Grind on grind
To stir the flesh
To squeeze the rind.

To mix the fruits
Till juices run
You are my moon
You are my sun.

This is my garden
I till to please
To bring delight
To bring you ease.

This is my temple
I worship here
Goddess love
Goddess care.

This is your bower
T'is where I serve
When duty calls
I serve with verve!

Hail Lady, I stand proudly
To serve I am not loath.
For in your garden of delights
I'm Master and Servant, both!

12th June 2008

Lotus

Lotus

The Lotus sits
Pure, pristine and symmetrical
Upon her murky seat.

The golden centre shining
Illuminating the creamy
White petals, from within.

I can imagine primitive man
Thinking that Godhead
Resided here, in this perfection.

I too, modern, sophisticated,
Twentieth century man
Trying on the twenty-first!.

Like a new overcoat
And rather liking
The fit and the feel of it.

I also feel, within this one
Perfect bloom
The touch of the Divine.

By whatever name
You choose
To call Her!

28th June 2008

Word From Oz

There's a whisper on the prairie
A word upon the "Ghan"
A murmur in the Outback
That they're at it again!

Yep, two who should know better
And who never meant no harm
But I do believe they're at it
Up in the Old Hay Barn.

They say they're talkin' literature
Among the bales and stooks
But that's the place for pleasure
Not discussing books!

But now I begin to wonder
Because we know our Jo is Boss
And a Book arrived this morning
And it's called a "Word From Oz."

And it's full of poems by Soma
It's full of words of delight
And the whisper's a Melbourne Bluesman
At last has got it right!

Written in loving memory of my dear
friend Phillip Barker of Melbourne,
AKA Cerberus or Soma Dog.
A great Bluesman and Poet. R.I.P.

18th July 2008

Weather Report

"There be squalls"
Here in Penzance
Chasing each other
Across roof-tops
Of houses and cars.

Dashing themselves
Into vapour
On all surfaces.
Death-sliding down
Roofs ~ over edges
Launders and gutters
Down-pipes overflowing.

Making raging rivers
In miniature
Down the steep streets
Leading to the sea.
Causing little dams
Of rubbish to form
Behind the wheels
Of Parked cars.

Last nights take away
Making a dash
For freedom
To evade
The hungry gulls.
School girls squeal
As each cold gust
Hits them
Too fashion conscious
To wear a coat
Or carry a 'brolly.

Visibility closes down
As each squall hits,
Opens again as sight
Follows the squall
Into the distance.
Across the bay.

cont.

And between each squall
Sunny spells shining
On the washed clean
Streets.

The street cleaners
Will be happy
All the rubbish
Is at the bottom
Of the hill!

18 Jan 2008

Chyandour Cliff

What'd you do if someone
Built a bloody great block of flats
Next door to your little cottage,
Have you ever thought of that?

What'd you do in the winter time
When you want a little fire?
You've just gotta go up on your roof
And build your chimney higher!

You don't want the fire smokin'
'Cos that'll just make you cough!
I bet when that bugger's drawin' well
It'd suck your socks right off!

16th May 2008

To be recited in the vernacular of Cornwall. This is the only two storey cottage I've ever
seen with a five storey chimney. I wonder who pays the chimney sweep?

Darkened Doorways

If upon a Golden Highway,
Darkened Doorways you espy,
Should you plumb those depths of darkness,
Or on heels made hasty - fly?

Could you find - within the darkness,
A Talisman or key which might,
Someday unlock a gate of Golden,
Into a City of Delight?

Could you lose yourself in darkness,
Lost to light and lost to day,
Or can you always keep some brightness,
In your soul to show the way?

It isn't always choice that throws us,
Into the abyss of despair,
But if you wave off the birds of sadness,
They can't nest there in your hair!

So, while you'd always choose the sunshine
Try to stick to that Highway bright,
The lessons most in need of learning,
Are often hidden in the night.

So Golden Highway, rocky road,
Or perilous crossing o'er the foam.
The only place that means safe harbour,
Will be the place you call home!

19 February 2008

Johnny Gurkha
(revised)

On the 11th September 2008, an 87 year old winner of the Victoria Cross, Britain's Highest Honour for Valour, RSM Tul Bahadur Pun VC, handed back his medals at the door of Number 10 Downing Street, the official residence of the Prime Minister, in protest at being denied medical treatment in a London hospital!

"Johnny Gurkha"

In utter disgust I write these words
I shouldn't have to write this letter
About a Comrade of mine, sold down the line
We should treat our old friends better.
* The War cry of the Gurkhas
In the rattle of the battle
In the fog of fusillade
There's a comrade I'd have beside me
And no better friend was made.

He's a Gurkha from the Mountains
I'd have watch my left and right
And stalwart stand, kukri in hand
And guard me day and night.

And when the battle's over
You forget those bloody miles
And what sticks most is your courtly host
And those gentle Gurkha smiles.

And now I hear them marching
To the door of Number 10
They've come to say, we saved your day
And you throw us away again.

Refused the right to Doctors
Refused the right to stay
They've been our friends, right to the ends
How can we serve 'em this way?

You can thank your Gods, whichever Gods
You choose, why even Kali

cont.

They politely ask, don't take you to task
Or shout "Ayo Gurkhali!"*

In every little skirmish,
In every war that's been
He's been our mate, since early date
In Eighteen Seventeen.

And now it's time to show the world
To lead by some example
To show these friends before it ends
Our gratitude is ample.

12th September 2008

This is dedicated with love and admiration to the men of 51 Gurkha Infantry Brigade and 99 Gurkha Infantry Brigade with whom I had the honour of serving during the Borneo Campaign. 1963 to 1966

*The War cry of the Gurkhas:

"Ayo Gurkhali" = "Here come the Gurkhas!" "Jai Mahakali, Ayo Gurkhali" = "Hail Goddess Kali. The Gurkhas are upon you!"

The well known actress Joanna Lumley, among others, waged a successful campaign to redress at least some of the outrageous treatment our old allies were subjected to. Bless her!

Cowboys and Indians or The Optimist

Many years ago
When I first moved
To the country
I worked on a farm.

On my way to work
I'd often come across
A traffic jam
In the country lane.

Godfrey walking behind
Ernie Hathams Cows
Re-enacting the film he'd seen
The previous night on TV.

One morning he would strut
Legs bowed from an evening
Bronc busting, hands hovering
Over his holstered colts.

Next day perhaps
With his rifle at the high port
He'd patrol the lane behind the cows
Wary head swivelling to find Germans in ambush.

When Godfrey became a Red Indian
Wellington boots lifting and shuffling
To the beat of the war dance
You kept tight hold of your scalp.

Every so often an advert would appear
In the local paper
"Wanted, Live in Housekeeper,
Apply, Godfrey,
The Caravan,
Ernie Hatham's Farm!"

22nd February 2008

Treat Our Soldiers Right

This piece was prompted by my learning that there are some 20,000 ex-servicemen in England and Wales either in Prison or on Probation for crimes largly associated with untreated Post Traumatic Stress Disorder. This is over twice the number of our troops currently serving in Afghanistan. For all I know the Government may consider this a cheaper option to treating and re-habilitating them!
I think it is a National Disgrace!

These are our 'boys' we're sending,
Sending off to war.
They'll come back changed,
They'll come back maimed,
Or they'll come back no more!

These are our 'boys' who're serving,
Serving in the fight.
They'll do their best,
To pass the test,
And do what we deem 'right'!

These are our 'boys' coming back,
Bearing tales they cannot tell!
They find that you don't understand,
Most will discard them out of hand,
And their Government will as well!

These are our 'boys' we send to jail,
Send them off right quick!
We've learned that men who suffer stress
Are better off in jail, no less!
Than being pampered on 'The Sick'!

It's bad enough we pay 'em,
To go and fight our part.
Cheaper far to jail 'em,
Than treat 'em for what ails 'em!
This Country, full of heart!

I weep for all the lost ones,
And those who're merely maimed!
But most of all I weep for us,

cont.

Who could treat our Soldiers thus?
Are you not ALL ashamed?

I say this to our Government,
Every Mothers son of you.
If you're not working day and night,
If you don't struggle to put this right,
Then you should be jailed too!

It's time we made a contract,
If we send our 'boys' to fight.
We should undo the damage done,
Relieve the stress earned by the gun.
And Treat Our Soldiers Right!

Treat Our Soldiers Right

2009

The Temple in the Lake

The Temple stands quiet
In the middle of the lake
Lonely in the mist

Ten thousand meditations
Leave only silence
The cobwebs of former lives

The mist leaves dew-drops
Like diamonds on every strand
Nature's offering

26th October 2009

A tribute to Kim Ki-Duc's Award Winning movie "Spring, Summer, Fall, Winter... and Spring"

Witch

Witch

You, my Witch
Are Magnificent
My hand is on yours
As we stir the retort
As you mix the potion
And cast the spell
To steal my soul.

In my heart
You stand tall
Against my stake
In the midst
Of my fire
Ablaze
But not burnt
Ablaze
But not consumed.

This morning
I was consumed
This morning
I burnt happily
In your blaze
Of Glory
And Beauty
And I know
This Morning.

You were
Consumed also.

23rd November 2007

To All In Durance Vile, Everywhere

To All In Durance Vile, Everywhere

A spot of sun
Head - high - on the wall
About the size of an open exercise book
Sloping upwards - left to right
I stand, facing the window
My back against the wall
Head in the sun
Feeling its warmth
On my skin.

The light shines golden orange
On my closed lids
Turning my world
To radiant warmth
Like the touch of God
Upon my face.

I forget my cold hands
Cold legs and feet
I bathe in warmth and light
The universe is warm and bright.
Like a womb
Taking me back to my
Microscopic origin
Whilst incubating the
Macroscopic destiny of all
I am as One.

The Universe swirls
The world turns
The sun spins
The shadows move
I shuffle crabwise along the wall
Remaining in the ray of light
As long as possible.

The sunbeam narrows
A foot long, a thin bar
On the wall

cont.

Still sloping
From left up to right
I stand with my head on one side
To catch the sun, as though listening
And I do listen
To the silence of the sun.

Now the spot of light
Is the size of a postage stamp
Just big enough to cover
One closed eye, still bathing it
With gold.
Half my world washed with sunlight
While darkness slowly spreads
Outward from my other eye.

The sunspot goes, I sway
Seeking it. It's gone.
Still with closed eyes
I sink to the floor where
Cross-legged, the cold returns
To my hands, my legs and feet
And I try to retain
The warmth, in my mind
And re-live upon my face
That gentle touch of God-
Until Tomorrow.

Written in the 1970's

After The Storm

Ah, the wind, the wind is dying,
As it puts the storm to bed,
In the sky the clouds are flying
As they chase each other o'erhead.

The halyards on the masts
Are quiet now they sleep,
When in the night they shrieked
Like Tormented from the deep.

The shore is piled high
With bladder wrack and weed
And in the rippling shallows
The swans still search for feed.

In the harbour they are bailing
Storm water from the boats
And the Ferry won't be sailing
Till we're wearing lighter coats.

They're sweeping shattered mast wood
From off the granite pier,
And three boats sank in Old St Ives
Across the land neck there.

In the park they use a chain saw
To cut up fallen trees
But after a storm like that
There'll be no more falling leaves.

The Fuchsia's at the Station
So bonnie just last week,
Are curled, burnt and shrivelled
From that storms salty reek

I've salt upon my windows,
Five hundred yards uphill
And though it's battered now and tattered
My flag is flying still.

2nd January 2008

The Condom Lectures

When my son was ten or eleven he came home, having spent the day at Lands End, a sort of Visitor Attraction, on the South West tip of Cornwall. A sort of Mini Disneyland of West Penwith!

I waited eagerly for news. The most startling of which was, "Dad, I've got a girl-friend now!"
"Oh really!" I replied, slightly taken aback, "What did you do all day?" Imagining playing on swings or some such. "We went on the Road-Train and did French-kissing!"

"Oh God/dess!" I thought, "It's not time for the Condom Lectures already, is it?" I knew my boy needed little instruction in the birds and the bees etc. He was country born and bred, neither of us would have thought twice about reaching out and helping a bull or a stallion with his "aim!" Proof positive, in my view that God must be a woman with a sense of humour. Had He been a man he would have given us something better to aim with!

Anyway. I decided rather than launch into the Condom Lectures unannounced I'd better enquire gently as to the extent of my son's interest in the opposite sex, i.e. how aroused he had become without embarrassing him with words like stiffie, woody or hard-on etc.

Very gently, with a finesse that amazed even me, I enquired how the experience of spending the day French-kissing a young maid had made him feel. After long and careful thought his reply delighted me, making me feel he was perhaps the perfect son and heir, to carry on my lifelong love-affair with the fairer sex.

"Well, Dad," he replied, "It did make me feel gentler!" God/dess I have always adored that child but at that moment he could do no wrong!.

Time passed and it eventually became time for the "Condom Lectures" in earnest. One day I was toiling up the last hill before dropping down into the valley where our little cottage nestled among the trees when I was overtaken by the school bus which screeched to a halt and out jumped my boy, getting off early to walk home with me. "Perfect moment, " I thought.

There was little embarrassment between us over things like that, but I felt I had to carefully state all the pros and cons of the situation and the need to be prepared, both for good manners, to prevent the chance of an unwanted pregnancy and to prevent the spread of sexually transmitted diseases.

I thought I'd covered all bases so I finished up by telling him that if he ever needed condoms I always had one in my wallet and there were some in my desk.

This boy, who was the apple of my eye and up to this moment had thought I was the most wonderful Dad in the world, hero of forgotten wars, tree climber extraordinaire, builder of the most thrilling Commando Slides in the district, repairer of scrambling motor cycles which could then be ridden cross-country to destruction again, then asked one more question. The one question that I hadn't anticipated, the question that heralded the end of the days of innocent childhood and the start of the teenage surly years!

"But Dad, why do you have condoms in your wallet and in your desk?" he asked.

"Well," I replied, "You never know, I might get lucky!"

"You'll never get lucky," he insisted, with all the worldly wisdom of a teenager, "You wear glasses!"

Oh, little did he know!

11th April 2008

Daniel and the Dinosaurs
A True Story

A few years ago, while my heart was still dying, before it was re-born to its present glory, I used to walk upon the beach between Penzance and Marazion early in the mornings. All weathers, all tides, walking, breathing, looking, watching, being.

One morning I found a message in a bottle, a plastic bottle that had reached the shore and blown up the sloping sand to the glacis breakwater. Here on this grey windswept shore a message. From where? From whom? How exciting, what opportunities lay in that tightly rolled piece of paper?

It took ages to winkle that piece of paper out of the bottle but when I did here is what I read.

"My name is Daniel, I am 4.
I go to Mousehole Play-school.
I like Dinosaurs.
My Favourite is the Triceratops."

Included on the paper in a more adult hand was Daniels full name and address.

He had obviously struggled with triceratops because he had been helped but apart from that he had obviously done everything else himself. I was so impressed, and particularly touched by his liking of the triceratops. Most boys would have gone for the T-Rex's or the other renders of flesh but here was a little boy who liked the triceratops, admittedly quite fierce looking but otherwise quite bovine. A grazer or a browser, almost the cow of the dinosaur world. I, who have spent much time being graced by the company of cattle, and who was for several years the district cow-lifter, liked that. A lot!

Any boy throwing a message in a bottle into the sea must have dreams of it being carried to strange and magic shores. Daniel just didn't need to know that his message, so carefully constructed had only crossed half way across Mounts Bay. This was a message in a bottle destined to cross oceans and land upon magic shores and to cross not only space but time as well. I conceived of a plan!

cont.

I searched the book stores of Penzance and finally discovered what I wanted.

I found a bed-time story book about dinosaurs, with pictures, where, as the story unfolded the dinosaurs came to life and all gathered round the bed of the boy in the story. The other book I found was a sort of Observers Book of Dinosaurs, a sort of Dictionary of Dinosaurs, an ideal first scientific book whose interest might possibly last Daniel for years.

All this I carefully packed into a neat parcel, I do do a neat parcel though I say so myself. Rather than include any explanation that an adult would take on board or misconstrue, I just included Daniels letter as an explanation, and also to cut loose the connection, because that wasn't what it was all about.

Then I did the unforgivable. I lied to an innocent. And this is the lie I told.

"Dear Daniel.
I Am very sorry to tell you this but
It took longer for your letter to reach the North
Pole than we expected. Your Christmas Present
Is therefore a little late. Thank you very much for your letter
and here are two books about your
Favourite subject. Lots of Love
Father Christmas"

Then I included this Lie in the parcel. And I posted it. Just like that. And the rest, as they say, is History! Or is that pre-history?

Occasionally, I wonder if there is an twelve year old boy called Daniel in Mousehole with an unshakable faith in Father Christmas. Or a young man well on his way to becoming a Palaeontologist or puzzled parents who are still wondering what's going on. But these are idle wonderings, I shall never seek to know because that is the pact made with the God of Giving. The not knowing is part of the delicious secret.

3rd December 2008

Bloody Moon

Lantern hanging in the trees,
Full moon overhead,
An orange moon, a bloody moon,
As I buried my dead!

She'd been a lover for many a year,
A friend so true and brave,
But under that bloody moon
I slaved to dig her grave.

A long-handled Cornish shovel
Digging in the night
The lantern swaying in the trees
Casting a ghastly light.

Tears flowed like salty rivers,
As I looked up at that moon,
I'd rather I'd been howling
Than sobbing like a loon.

I dug that grave so deep and wide,
As far as I could go,
And then I went and fetched her
To lay her down below.

I laid her down in that cold earth,
And shovelled in the soil,
And tears fell upon the sod,
As I finished up my toil.
Lantern hanging in the trees,
Full moon looks down scowling
An orange moon, a bloody moon,
I swear I heard it howling!

I placed some stones above her,
To hold her where she lay,
And whispered to her, as oft before,
'Lobo. Good Dog! Stay!'

7th February 2008

A Hill Of Chamomile

My Lady often teases me, about her wild hair style
Something she often likens, to a hill of chamomile.
But I always tell her, she can tease and tease and tease
But she is right up there, with cows and dogs and trees.

I'm very fond of cattle, I love their bovine grace,
Their slow deep wisdom and their relaxed and easy pace,
And dogs, oh don't you love 'em, they are so pleasurable to please
Why, they are right up there, with my girl and cows and trees!

And trees are oh so special, slow growing but oh so giving,
Among the very oldest things that are on this planet living.
Without them we would be in caves, no building without logs
Why, they are right up there, with my girl and cows and dogs!

So my Lady do not feel , that I would take you lightly,
My love for you is warm and strong, you make me feel quite sprightly,
You do not need to worry about the where's and why's and how's,
Why you're right up there in my heart, with trees and dogs and cows.

14th February 2009

Social Services or A Helping Hand

Ring Ring

"Hello, is that Social Services?"

"This is Social Services
Your call is in a queue,
Your call is important to us,
An advisor will answer your call,
As soon as one is available.
Or you can call back when
We are not so busy!"

Muzac

"Social Services.
How may I help you?"

"Hello.
Is that the Department
That issues disabled aids
To disabled Old Soldiers?"

"What is your name?"

"My name is John B.... you came..."

"What is your number?"

"01736 3....."

"Not your telephone number, your number!"

"2392....."

"That is not your number either!"

"I can assure you it is.
A good soldier
Never forgets his number!
I know, I've got it right here,   cont.

Engraved round the edge,
Of this medal they gave me,
That I cut into a Love and Peace Sign
As soon as I got out!"

"I want your National Insurance number,
It starts with two letters!"

"Oh! Then you only had to ask,
There is no point in snapping at me!
I'm not here for my health, you know!
Ah, here it is.... Zulu X-ray 14...."

"Mr B.... will you stop going
Off on tangents and give me
Your National Insurance number!"

"I was, I said......."

"I know perfectly well what you said,
You started talking about Zulu's!"

"That was the Phonetic Alphabet,
Used the world over
For ease of Communication!
If only it worked here!
My number is zed ex......"

"What's that?"

"Zed ex........"

WHATTTTT!"

"Zulu X-ray........"

"Ah! At last!"

"Zulu X-ray 14.. Etc etc!"

"Right Mr B.... that wasn't so difficult,
Was it?
Now what can we do for you?"   cont.

"Well, you know those sorta snappy things,
With jaws that help you pick things up,
When you can't bend very well?"

"We call those 'snappy' things,
'Helping Hands.' Mr B...."

"Ah! Yes, helping hands!
Could I have another one.
Please."

"Another one! Another one!
We gave you a helping hand,
Two years ago. Why on earth,
Would you want another one?"

"Well, you see,
It is a little awkward.
When I want to use it
Upstairs,
It's Downstairs!
And when I want to use it,
Downstairs,
It's Upstairs!
If I had two........!"

"Two! Two!
You are not allowed two!
Why can't you go upstairs
And fetch it?"

"Erm...... Because
I'm disabled?"

"You have no idea
How many times
I hear that excuse!
One! You are allowed
One! Under no circumstances
Are you allowed two!
The only time we ever
Issue another one,
Is when   cont.

You've worn
The other one
Out!
Goodbye!"

Ring ... ring
(At this point
You may repeat most
Of the previous conversation...
Or you can take it as read!)

"Hello, Social Services
I've broken my Helping Hand.
Can I have another one?"

"That is another department
Mister B......
I'm putting you through!"

Ring ... ring(At this point....etc...etc)

Why is it that dealing with
The Government,
Or it's Minions,
Makes Liars of us all?

19th September 2009

The Headhunter's Daughter

Her hair, blue-black and silky,
Hung down to her waist,
Her breasts, pert, round and perfect,
Were exactly to her taste.

As sweet and soft as wild hibiscus,
A maiden to her core,
A short sarong from hip to knee,
Was all she usually wore.

A hundred gods had laboured
On the perfection of her face.
And her steps were slow and graceful,
With seduction in every pace.

Washed clean in jungle rivers,
Kissed by the tropic sun,
She was the sweetest thing of fifteen years,
And her life had just begun!

She chose her lover wisely,
Sleek and sure as a jungle cat!
And all the young men thought about,
Was to share her sleeping mat!

And when she was quite certain,
With touch and glances long,
She lured him to her bedside,
And opened her sarong!

And when she was quite certain,
And happy with her choice,
She let him love her one more time,
And gave her thoughts a voice!

"You have given me much pleasure,
I know the same is true for you.
I feel life start within my belly,
As it's supposed to do.

Now early in the morning,

cont.

Get up 'n' leave my bed!
And prove to me you are a man!
And Go! Fetch me a HEAD!"

3rd October 2009

Dedicated to the so-called Headhunting Tribes of Borneo.

Delightful people, warm and friendly, provided you weren't an enemy! They were bright and intelligent and extremely sophisticated in living their jungle lives. The children were unspoiled and were mostly delightfully polite and I never heard a voice nor saw a hand raised against them!

Their young ladies were renowned for their beauty and their generous natures. But sad to say, it was usually them who sent the men off to take a head or two!

Kerouac

What does Kerouac mean to me?

Riding the Sunburned Thumb to Oblivion!

The sheer exuberance of being able to carry one's own pack,
To hump one's bluey, dog eared copy of "On the Road"
Slowly dissolving to dust in a jeans back pocket.
Not exactly showing me the road
I'd been travelling since aged fifteen
But the first hint that there were others
Seeking far horizons for no other reason
Than they were there!

Apart from traditional travelling people
And those salt of the earth travelling Irish
Looking for the next ditch to dig
The next road to build
All of whom had cheerfully shared their fire with me
And their work with me.
Apart from those Kerouac was
The first to say to me,
"You are not alone out there!"
Despite the gentle hum of silence!

8th October 2009

The Down 'Omers or The Angels of Wan Chai

They were the flowers of their poverty,
The prettiest of the weeds.
The need to eat and support themselves,
Would often shape their deeds.
But when British Troops lay bleeding,
In foreign streets so far,
T'was the Angels of Wan Chai,
Showed what real ladies are!

They'd enter short term contracts,
With soldiers posted there.
They'd keep his board and keep his bed,
And be his wife out there.
And as long as the posting lasted,
They'd cleave close to his side,
And when the troopship sailed away,
They'd be someone else's bride.

"funny an' yellow and faithful,
Doll in a teacup, she were,
But we lived on the square,
Like a true married pair,
An' I learned about women from her!"

"Where're you going, Tommy?"
You might ask as he left camp.
"Down 'ome!" was often his reply,
As downhill he would stamp.
So "Down 'omers" they became,
Those flowers of the night,
And while Tommy treated 'em decent,
They'd always treat 'im right!

The memsahib looked down on them,
As nothing but sluts and whores.
But the memsahib looked down on Tommy,
Those pale insipid bores!
But while they were complaining,
How hard the war was on the wives,
T'was the Angels of the gutter,
Went out and saved some lives!

cont.

When the memsahib in Singapore,
Were bribing passage for a few,
The Angels of Wan Chai,
Went were the bullets flew,
They carried food and medicine,
To the defenders of Hong Kong,
They bandaged up the wounded,
All night and all day long!

And when the fight was over,
That Christmas the wounded lay,
Out in the streets for 'most a week,
And were tended every day.
By Angels in silk cheongsams,
Skin tight and split to thigh,
Who braved the bullets and the rape,
That Tommy wouldn't die!

British and Canadian,
Indian Soldiers lost,
Were rounded up like cattle,
And into jail tossed!
And in all the years of hardship,
The Wan Chai Angels threw,
Food and meds across the wire,
To try and save a few!

They were the flowers of their poverty,
The prettiest of the weeds.
The need to eat and support themselves,
Would often shape their deeds!
But when Commonwealth Troops lay bleeding,
In foreign streets so far,
T'was the Angels of Wan Chai,
Showed what real ladies are!

24th October 2009

Written in honour of the Angels of Wan Chai, whose actions during and after the fall of
Hong Kong saved the lives of many Commonwealth Troops. Lest we forget!
The verse in italics is stolen, quite shamelessly, from my friend Rudyard Kipling!

Bow Music

The old man plays his bow
And dreams of the young maid
The young maid listens to his music
And dreams of a young man.

But the music has but one desire
The perfection of the melody!

29th October 2009

Inspired by Kim Ki-Duk's film "The Bow"

Pipa Music

From under the tea-house eaves
Pipa music lifts it's exquisite voice
And wafts up the mountainside

To where the Gods sit smiling
And gently tap their feet!

30th October 2009

Inspired by my friend Liu Fang's beautiful music

The Paso Doble

These tired old feet
Dragging their ass
Down these grey streets.

But my heart tells them
They can still dance
The paso doble!

30th October 2009

The Pipa Player

The right hand plucks
The music from the strings.

The left, pushing, sliding, caressing
Bestows it's soul.

She holds her instrument
Like a lover or a baby.

But it is the heart and soul
Of the pipa player

Meditating with her instrument
That sings and soars to heaven!

2nd November 2009

Inspired by the wonderful music of my dear friend Liu Fang.

Huà Shàn Mountain

Pilgrimage to Hua Shan Mountain
Beside me a rock face and a rusty chain,
Beneath me, three planks and the eternal wind.

No wonder they thought Taoists immortal.
Come this way once and you'll think
You can live forever!

5th November 2009

I Expect No Less

I Expect No Less.

Am I not worthy of all that a Year Book may contain?
And all that the intervening years have written
Upon your lovely face and your beloved body?
And I too have a story to write upon your bones,
And to scribe with kisses upon your skin!

Drink tea, bathe, prepare a clean and fragrant parchment
I have tales of love and surrender to write upon your soul,
Tales of lust and plunder to implant within your belly,
Tales of love and comfort to quiet your mind.
Tales of love and tenderness to enfold your heart!

You smell of lotus and brown sugar let me breathe you in,
Let me worship at the Altar of the Woman you became,
The prophecy you wrote of, it nearly did come true
Because you make love just like a Woman
But you sleep just like a little girl.

8th December 2007

Injured Birds

Injured birds break my heart
Like injured innocence
Losing the gift of flight

If only one could cradle
Them in warm palms
Heal with the touch of love

Breath fresh confidence
Into their timid breasts
Their recovery would mend my heart!

13th April 2008

Index

MAPublisher Catalogue

ISBN/Titles /Image/Author	ISBN/Titles /Image/Author	ISBN/Titles /Image/Author	ISBN/Titles /Image/Author
978-1-910499-00-9 Father to child By Mayar Akash	978-1-910499-08-5 HSJ Lakri Tura By Mayar Akash	978-1-910499-26-9 Colouring 1-10 By MAPublisher	978-1-910499-18-4 Basic Numbers 1-10 By MAPublisher
978-1-910499-16-0 River of Life By Mayar Akash	978-1-910499-09-2 HSJ Gilaf Procession By Mayar Akash	978-1-910499-27-6 Activity Numbers 1-10 By MAPublisher	978-1-910499-19-1 Number 1-100 By MAPublisher
978-1-910499-39-9 Eyewithin By Mayar Akash	978-1-910499-03-0 HSJ Mazar Sharif By Mayar Akash	978-1-910499-28-3 Activity Colouring Alphabets By MAPublisher	978-1-910499-20-7 Vowels By MAPublisher
978-1-910499-32-0 WG Survivor By Mayar Akash	978-1-910499-06-1 Hazrat Shahjalal By Mayar Akash	978-1-910499-68-9 The Adventures of Sylheti mazars By Mayar Akash	978-1-910499-21-4 Alphabet Consonants By MAPublisher
978-1-910499-66-5 Yesteryears By Mayar Akash	978-1-910499-07-8 HSJ Urus By Mayar Akash	978-1-910499-38-2 Bite Size Islam: 99 Names of Allah By Mayar Akash	978-1-910499-22-1 Vowels & Short By MAPublisher

ISBN/Titles /Image/Author	ISBN/Titles /Image/Author	ISBN/Titles /Image/Author	ISBN/Titles /Image/Author
978-1-910499-15-3 Anthology One By Penny Authors	978-1-910499-36-8 Delirious By Liam Newton	978-1-910499-52-8 Lit From Within By Ruth Lewarne	978-1-910499-57-3 The Vampire of the Resistance By Ruth Lewarne
978-1-910499-17-7 Anthology Two By Penny Authors	978-1-910499-54-2 Book of Lived v6 Penny Authors	978-1-910499-49-8 Cry for Help By B. M. Gandhi	978-1-910499-55-9 Riversolde By Meriyon
978-1-910499-29-0 Book of Lived v3 By Penny Authors	978-1-910499-37-5 When You Look Back By Rashma Mehta	978-1-910499-14-6 The Halloweeen Poem by Zainab Khan	978-1-910499-70-2 Smiley & The Acorn By Roger Underwood
978-1-910499-351 V4 Book of Lived By Penny Authors	978-1-910499-37-5 My Dream World By Rashma Mehta	978-1-910499 69 6 Consciousness By Mustak Mustafa	978-1-910499-40-5 World's First University By Giasuddin Ahmed
978-1-910499-50-4 Book of Lived v5 By Penny Authors	978-1-910499-53-5 Angel Eyez By Rashma Mehta	978-1-910499-73-3 Book of Lived v7 By Penny Authors	978-1-910499-56-6 The Warrior Queen By Giasuddin Ahmed

www.mapublisher.org.uk

ISBN/Titles /Image/Author	ISBN/Titles /Image/Author	ISBN/Titles /Image/Author	ISBN/Titles /Image/Author
978-1-910499-58-0 Tower Hamlets, Random, One Mayar Akash	978-1-910499-60-3 Tower Hamlets, Random, Two By Mayar Akash	978-1-910499-05-4 Tide of Change By Mayar Akash	978-1-910499-51-1 Brick & Mortar By Mayar Akash
978-1-910499-61-0 Grenfell Tower By Mayar Akash	978-1-910499-63-4 Power Houses By Mayar Akash	978-1-910499-71-9 Altab Ali Murder By Mayar Akash	978-1-910499-31-3 Pathfinders By Mayar Akash
978-1-910499-62-7 Community Service 1992-1993 By Mayar Akash	978-1-910499-64-1 Bancroft Estate By Mayar Akash	978-1-910499-11-5 Re-Awakening By Mayar Akash	978-1-910499-13-9 Chronicle of Sylhetis of UK By Mayar Akash
978-1-910499-59-7 Brick Lane, Spitalfields By Mayar Akash	978-1-910499-72-6 25th Anniversary of Bangladesh By Mayar Akash	978-1-910499-12-2 Young Voice Mayar Akash	978-1-910499-42-9 Bangladeshi Fishes By Mayar Akash
978-1-910499-65-8 PYO Polish Exchange 1992 By Mayar Akash	978-1-910499-30-6 TH Bangladeshi Politicians By Mayar Akash	978-1-910499-10-8 Vigil Subotaged By Mayar Akash	978-1-910499-67-2 F. Ahmed and History By Mukid Choudhury

www.mapublisher.org.uk

ISBN/Titles /Image/Author	ISBN/Titles /Image/Author	ISBN/Titles /Image/Author	ISBN/Titles /Image/Author
978-1-910499-43-6 My Life Book 1 By Mayar Akash	978-1-910499-44-3 My Life Book 2 By Mayar Akash	978-1-910499-45-0 My Life Book 3 By Mayar Akash	978-1-910499-46-7 My Life Book 4 By Mayar Akash
978-1-910499-47-4 My Life Book 5 By Mayar Akash	978-1-910499-75-7 Bangladeshis in Manchester - Oral History, Part 1 By M.A. Mustak	978-1-910499-74-0 Peter Fox Artist (LE) A Re-enchantment of Contemporary Art By Peter Fox	978-1-910499-78-8 On The Seventh Day By Cosette Ratliff
978-1-910499-79-5 Altab Ali Life & Family By Mayar Akash	978-1-910499-77-1 Smiley & the Acorn Treasure on the Isles of Scilly By Roger Underwood	978-1-910499-80-1 India – stories from the Banyan Tree Paul Wadsworth	978-1-910499-84-9 V8 Book of lived Penny Authors
978-1-910499-87-0 Behind the tears Rashma Mehta	978-1-910499-85-6 RhythmScripts My Feet is just mine Libby Pentreath	978-1-910499-89-4 Podgy and the Delightful Company John Dillon	978-1-910499-90-0 Calm and the Storm Alison Norton
9781910499887 Pebble Libby Pentreath	9781910499917 The Crab's Tale John Dillon	9781910499924 Res Burman's Poetry V1 Res J. F. Burman	9781910499931 Res Burman's Poetry V2 Res J. F. Burman

www.mapublisher.org.uk

ISBN/Titles /Image/Author	ISBN/Titles /Image/Author	ISBN/Titles /Image/Author	ISBN/Titles /Image/Author
9781910499962 Lowry's Boats Roger Lowry	9781910499979 Who is? Tilesky Mayar Akash	9781910499238 The Symbol Mayar Akash	9781910499245 Montol Mayar Akash
9781910499962 Time & Tide Rob Kersley	9781910499986 The Departure Lounge Tyrone Mark Warren	9781910499252 The Shipwreck of my Past Robert Cardwell-Spencer	9781910499xxx She Poetry Penny Authors
Words of Frost Adrian Frost	Tim's Collection St Michael's bay 140 years on the cards	Cornish Poets Penny Authors	

.

www.ingramcontent.com/pod-product-compliance
Lightning Source LLC
LaVergne TN
LVHW051704080426

835511LV00017B/2725